Delicious Pork Recipes For Your Kitchen

Destiny A. Busby

Delicious Pork Recipes For Your Kitchen : Mouthwatering Pork Dishes to Elevate Your Home Cooking Game

Funny helpful tips:

Respect each other's space; individual time is essential for personal growth.

Stay informed about the evolution of e-learning platforms; they're democratizing education globally.

Introduction

This book is the perfect companion for novice cooks eager to explore the versatility of pork in their culinary adventures. From grilling and smoking to stovetop cooking and using Instant Pot or crockpot methods, this cookbook covers a wide range of techniques and recipes to help beginners master the art of cooking pork.

Before diving into the recipes, readers are introduced to essential information about pork, including tips on selecting cuts, understanding cooking methods, and ensuring safe handling practices in the kitchen.

The cookbook features an array of mouthwatering recipes, starting with simple yet flavorful dishes like Easy Pork Loin, Apple Pork Chops, and Caribbean Fajitas. These recipes provide a solid foundation for beginners to build their confidence in cooking pork.

For those interested in barbecue and smoking techniques, the cookbook offers tantalizing options such as Hickory Pulled Pork, Smoked Butt, and Apple Pork Butt, along with homemade BBQ sauce recipes to complement the flavors of the meat.

Stovetop cooking enthusiasts will find recipes like Juicy Pan-Fried Chops, Pork Ginger Stir-Fry, and Italian Pork Chops with Roasted Potatoes, providing quick and easy meal solutions without the need for specialized equipment.

The Instant Pot and crockpot section introduces convenient methods for preparing pork, including Instant Pot Spicy Pork Tacos, Instant Pot Pork Puttanesca, and Chunked Pork Over Zucchini Spirals, perfect for busy individuals looking to streamline meal preparation.

From breakfast options like Breakfast Flatbread to hearty mains like Pork Enchiladas and Pork & Beans Tater Tot Casserole, the cookbook offers a diverse range of recipes to suit every palate and occasion.

Each recipe is accompanied by clear instructions, helpful tips, and vibrant photographs, making it easy for beginners to follow along and create delicious pork dishes with confidence. With this book, aspiring cooks can embark on a flavorful journey and discover the joys of cooking with pork.

Contents

Things to Know About Pork

1. Always thaw before cooking then pat dry with paper towels.
2. To avoid dry pork, sear the fat on fatty cuts over high heat before cooking at a lower heat.
3. Slow braising, slow cooking or stewing are ways of getting moist, tender meat.
4. Belly, neck, and shoulder are the fattiest cuts and are best suited for slow-cooking, roasting, braising.
5. Shoulder is best for pulled pork.
6. Lean pork cuts come from the loin and include chops and medallions.
7. For leaner cuts consider keeping the bone in, it helps keep the meat juicy.
8. Try slow cooking certain lean cuts like the leg. This keeps meat juicy.
9. Brining helps to infuse meat with flavor and breakdown connective tissues; however, this practice is reserved for larger pieces such as ham, ribs, and sometimes bellies. Smaller pieces of meat like chops and loins are marinated.
10. To tenderize- cut down muscle fiber- first put piece between two strips of clear wrap then hammer into an even piece.
11. Marinades are your friends; they infuse and can tenderize depending on acidity levels!
12. Depending on size of meat marinade 25 minutes to 48 hours.
13. When marinating large pieces score top so liquids can penetrate down and flavor the meat inside.
14. A tenderized cut that is boneless, breaded, and fried is an escalope or schnitzel.

15.15.

Lean pieces tend to dry out, so consider wrapping in other meats such as bacon!

16. In skillet or pot, always keep meats at least ½-1-inch apart. This ensures flavorfull, even cooking.

17. Tips for great spareribs: brine; take off the skin's outer membrane before seasoning; bring them up to room temperature; and finally, baste with rib juices or marinade to keep meat from drying out.

Grill/Smoker

Grilling tips:

1. Always bring meat to room temp before grilling. This helps reduce shrinking.
2. Always season with salt and pepper while bringing to room temp. The salt & pepper will burn off during cooking but brings out the internal juices of the meat!
3. Clean the grate.
4. Do not overmix or over-handle it dries out the meat.
5. Before forming burgers dampen your hands with water to avoid meat sticking and clumping to hands.
6. Do not start cooking until grill has reached full heat. A trick for telling this is if you can hold your hand 4-5 inches above grate and count to 5.
7. Resist the urge to press the patties! This pushes out its juices.
8. Pork, beef and lamb burgers should reach 160°. Turkey or chicken burgers should be cooked to 165°.
9. Try to cook first by time then by temperature. Cutting into meat allows juices to escape.
10. Let meat sit 7-10 minutes to allow juices to redistribute.
11. Press thumb into the middle of patty to prevent sinking in the middle.

Pork Meat Cuts

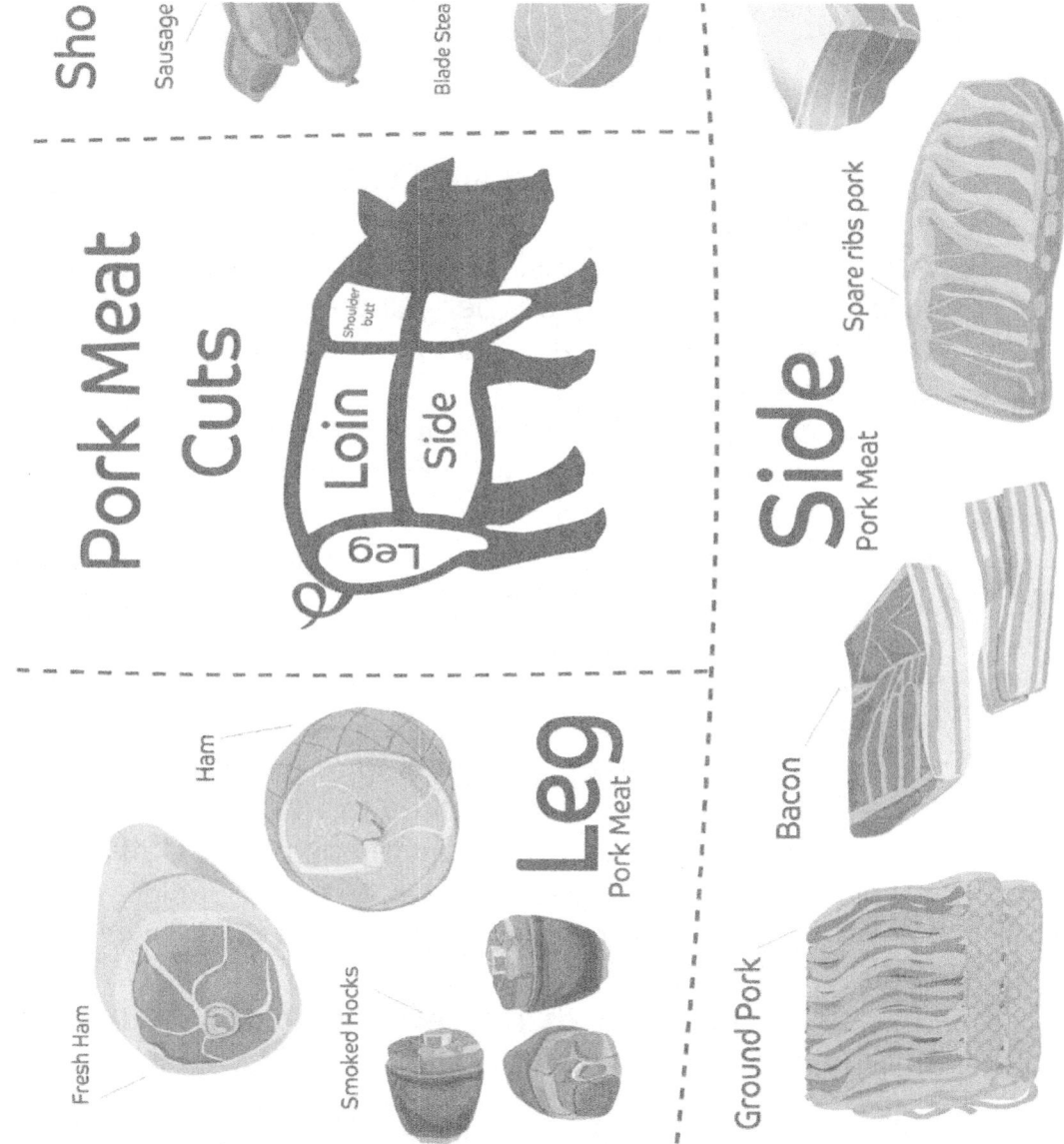

Sho
- Sausage
- Blade Stea

Leg
Pork Meat

- Ham
- Fresh Ham
- Smoked Hocks

Side
Pork Meat

- Spare ribs pork
- Bacon
- Ground Pork

Easy Pork Loin

Use flavored wood! Makes 1 3-5-pound loin.

Ingredients:

- 1 3-5-lb loin
- 3/4 tbsp brown sugar
- 2/3 tsp garlic, minced
- ½ tbsp onion, minced
- 4-6 whole cloves
- 2 tbsp thick steak sauce (Heinz 57 sauce)
- 1/3 tsp cinnamon
- 1/4 cup honey
- 1 tsp Worcestershire

Directions:

In a bowl combine brown sugar, minced ginger, minced garlic, minced ginger, minced onion, steak sauce, cinnamon, honey, Worcestershire sauce together. Push cloves into tenderloin.

Pour half of marinade in plastic bag with tenderloin and let sit in refrigerator 4 hours to overnight.

Grill over medium-high heat 30-45 minutes.

Brushing occasionally with remaining marinade.

Apple Pork Chops

Try all flavors of wood chips! Makes 2 servings.

Ingredients:

- 2 center cut pork chops
- ½ tbsp lemon peel
- 2 sprigs parsley
- 1/3 tsp cinnamon
- 1/5 tsp nutmeg
- Apple wood chips

Directions:

Spread 1-2 cups wood chips on fire (or as directed on package).

In plastic bag combine pork chops, lemon peel, parsley, cinnamon, nutmeg and marinate over night.

Remove, pat dry, grill over medium-high heat 5-9 minutes per side until reaching 145 degrees F.

Pork Spareribs and a Homemade BBQ Sauce

Try low sodium soy sauce instead of Worcestershire sauce! Makes 1-2 slabs.

Ingredients:

- 1-2 slabs pork ribs
- 1 tbsp Worcestershire sauce
- 1/3 cup brown sugar
- 1 1/3 cups ketchup
- 1/2 cup distilled white vinegar
- 1/4 cup honey
- 1/2 tsp ginger
- 1/2 tsp sea salt

- ½ tbsp dry mustard
- 1/2 tsp garlic powder and parsley
- 1/3 tsp white pepper

Directions:

In a sauce pot over medium heat mix together ketchup, brown sugar, white vinegar, honey, Worcestershire sauce, ginger, salt, mustard, garlic powder and parsley, pepper, and stock.

Next, bring to boil, cover, reduce heat and simmer 25-30 minutes stirring occasionally.

Grill ribs over medium heat 60-90 minutes.

Brushing once with sauce after 45 minutes then again 1-2 minutes before being done.

Lastly, remove from heat, brush with sauce, let cool 10 minutes before cutting

Asparagus with Rosemary Chops

Try them with Italian oregano or lemon thyme. Makes 4 servings.

Ingredients:

- 4 center cut pork chops
- ¼ cup olive oil
- 1/2 tbsp lemon juice
- 1/2 tbsp Worcestershire sauce
- 1/4 tbsp spicy mustard
- 1/3 tbsp oregano
- 1 tsp onion powder
- 2/3 tsp garlic powder
- 1/3 tsp pepper
- 1/2 tbsp diced rosemary for topping
- 6-8 asparagus spears

- 1-2 tomatoes, quartered
- Extra virgin olive oil

Directions:

In plastic bag combine chops, olive oil, lemon juice, Worcestershire sauce, spicy mustard, oregano, onion, garlic powder, pepper, and marinade in refrigerator overnight.

Remove, pat dry, bring to room temperature.

Grill over medium-high 5-8 minutes per side depending on thickness.

Transfer chops to plate and sprinkle with rosemary.

Layout sheet of foil.

Place quartered tomatoes down and drizzle with e.v.o.o.

Lay asparagus spears on grill and drizzle with oil.

Cook 4-5 minutes over medium-high heat.

Caribbean Fajitas

Great meat for soups, stews, sandwich's, and stir-fries! Makes 6 fajitas.

Ingredients:

- 1 3-pound pork tenderloin
- 1 tbsp onion, minced
- 2/3 tbsp lime juice
- ½ tsp garlic, minced
- 1 red pepper, diced
- 1 jalapeno, diced
- ½ cup crushed pineapple
- 1/3 cup washed black beans
- 2 tbsp olive oil
- 1 tbsp brown sugar

- 1/3 tbsp Caribbean jerk seasoning
- 6 corn or flour 8-inch fajita shells

Directions:

Whisk together onion, lime juice, minced garlic, brown sugar, Caribbean jerk seasoning.

Submerge tenderloin in marinade.

Next, cover and place in refrigerator 4 hours to overnight.

Cook pork 35-45 minutes, remove, and let cool.

Meanwhile combine red pepper, jalapeno, crushed pineapple, olive oil, and black beans.

Then, warm tortillas 30 seconds – 1 minute per side.

Fill warm tortillas with pork and top with salsa, enjoy!

Chops & Noodles

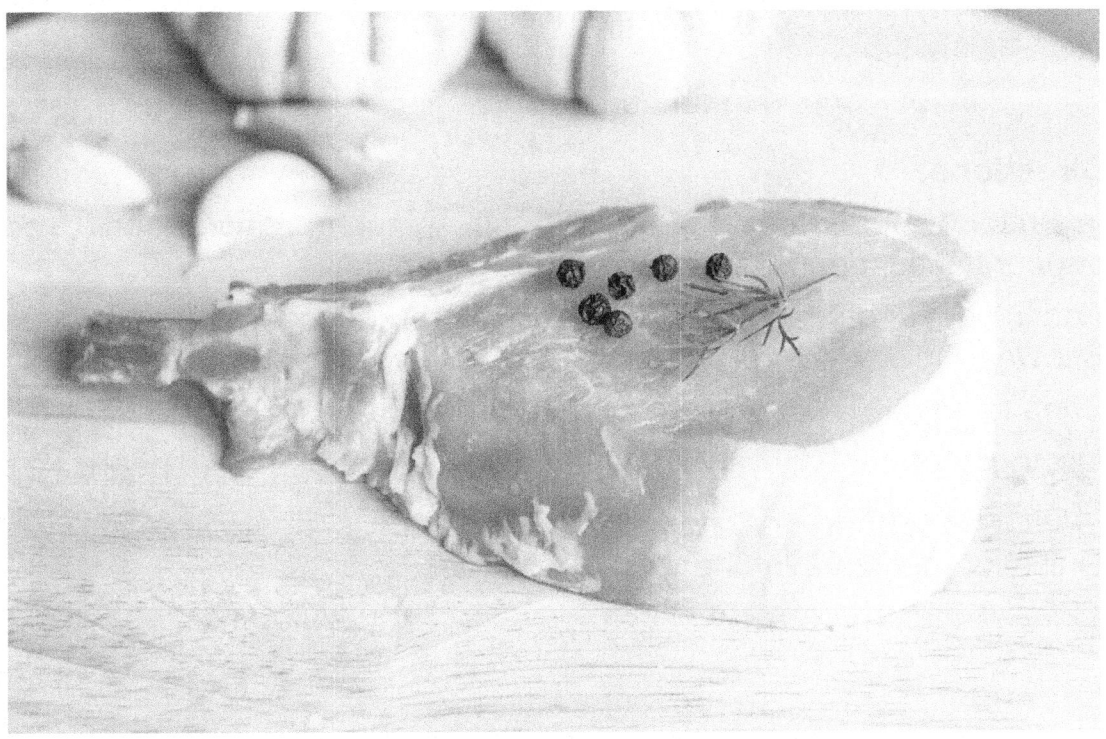

Makes great leftovers! Makes 4 chops.

Ingredients:

- 4 pork chops
- ½ tsp pepper
- 1/2 tsp garlic powder
- 2 tsp sweet ginger
- 3/4 tsp smoked paprika
- 2 tsp sesame oil
- ½ tbsp olive oil
- 1/4 cup finely chopped kale, washed
- 1 tsp garlic, minced
- 1 tsp red pepper flakes (optional)
- 1 cup low sodium garbanzo or blackbeans

- 1 cup edamame or green/yellow beans
- 1 cup chicken or veggie stock (water works too)
- 1 cup worth rice noodles, uncooked
- ½ package tofu
- 2 tbsp chopped fresh herbs

Directions:

In Dutch oven add sesame oil, olive oil, spinach , minced garlic, red pepper flakes, beans, stock and sauté 1 minute.

Add in cubed tofu, edamame, stock or water, uncooked rice noodles. Stir well.

Bring to a boil. Then, cover and reduce heat. Let simmer 20-25

Mix together pepper, garlic powder, sweet ginger, smoked paprika.

Sprinkle on chops.

Grill over medium-high heat 10-12 minutes.

Easy Chops & Tater Wedges

For softer wedges, boil the potatoes for 5 minutes first. Makes 4 servings.

Ingredients:

- 4 center cut pork chops
- ¾ cup olive oil
- 2/3 tsp red wine vinegar
- 2/3 tbsp Italian oregano, diced
- 4 balls mozzarella cheese OR provolone cheese
- 1-2 large sweet potatoes
- Extra virgin olive oil
- Sweet paprika
- ½ tsp cumin
- ½ tsp chili powder

- 1 tsp dried rosemary

Directions:

Wash and cut sweet potato into wedges.

Mix together sweet paprika, cumin, chili powder, dried rosemary.

Sprinkle over sweet potato wedges.

For vinaigrette, whisk together olive oil, red wine vinegar, Italian oregano. Cover and chill.

Over medium-high flame cook porkchops 5 minutes on one side. Flip and cook 5 minutes.

During last minute top each with cheese, let melt.

Lay sheet of aluminum foil on grate.

Lay wedges out and drizzle with olive oil.

Cook wedges 5-7 minutes, flip, repeat.

Transfer chops to plates, divide fries amongst them, top chops with vinaigrette.

Italian Pork Roast

Great meat for soups, stews, and casseroles. Makes 1 pork roast

Ingredients:

- 1 pork roast
- ½ quart unsalted beef broth
- 1 chopped bell pepper- or- chili oil
- 1 chopped onion
- 1 tbsp minced garlic
- ½ tsp sea salt
- ½-2/3 tbsp sugar or brown sugar

Directions:

In a large pot combine broth, red pepper flakes or oil, onion, garlic, sea salt, sugar or brown sugar; turn on heat and bring to gentle boil stirring until sugars dissolve

Remove from heat and let cool completely then drop in pork roast and refrigerate 2-3 hours

Set grill for 200 and smoke 7-8 hours

pour some brine mixture into water pan of grill setup

Hickory Pulled Pork

Makes excellent sandwiches. Makes 1 pork roast

Ingredients:

- 1 pork roast
- 1 cup apple cider vinegar
- 1 tbsp brown sugar
- ½ tbsp black pepper

Directions:

In a large bowl combine pork roast, a.c.v., pepper and sit in refrigerator 2-4 hours

Set grill to 200 and grill 7-8 hours using hickory chips mixed in the charcoal

Smoked Butt

When buying pork, look for minimal fat and healthy part. Makes 1 pork butt

Ingredients:

- 1 pork butt
- ½ cup low sodium apple juice
- 1 tsp garlic juice (juice from jar of minced garlic)
- 1 tbsp brown sugar
- 1 tsp low sodium soy sauce

Directions:

Whisk together apple juice, garlic juice, brown sugar, soy sauce until sugar dissolves and inject into multiple sites; without fully removing needle arrange to different angles dispersing liquid through butt

Wrap in clear wrap then sit in refrigerator or put on ice for 4 hours to overnight; Remove, dry, let sit 25-45 minutes

Set grill temp to 225 and start smoking until temp of 195 is reached

Apple Pork Butt

Some of the most tender mouthwatering pork you will ever have!
Makes 1 pork butt

Ingredients:

- 1 pork butt
- ½ cup apple juice
- 1/4 cup apple cider vinegar
- 1 tbsp Worcestershire sauce
- ½ tbsp brown sugar
- ½ cup apple juice
- 1/3 cup molasses
- 1 tsp cayenne pepper
- ¼ tsp cloves
- 1/3 tsp dry mustard

Directions:

In bowl combine ½ cup apple juice, a.c.v., Worcestershire sauce, brown sugar; stir until sugar dissolves; let sit in refrigerator 4 hrs. to overnight

Set grill temp to 200 and cook 3 hours

Combine apple juice, molasses, cayenne pepper, cloves and baste butt with mixture every 30 minutes

Continue cooking and basting for another 3-5 hours

Pork Belly/Pastrami

Makes delicious sandwiches. Makes 1 pastrami/pork belly

Ingredients:

- 1 pork belly
- 3-4 cups water
- 1 tbsp kosher salt
- 2 tbsp mirin
- 1 tbsp coriander seeds
- 1 tbsp allspice
- 1 mustard seeds
- 1 cinnamon
- 1 tsp ginger powder
- 1 tbsp peppercorn
- ½ tbsp brown sugar

- 1 bay leaf

Directions:

In a pan toast coriander seeds, allspice, mustard seeds, cinnamon, ginger, peppercorn, brown sugar 1-2 minutes or until very fragrant

In bowl or large pot combine toasted spices, water, Mirin, bay leaf, and pork belly; sit in refrigerator 4 hours to overnight

Set grill temp to 225 and cook 6-8 hours

-for extra flavor pour some brine in water pan

N.C. Pig

Any beer will work! Makes 1 pork butt

Ingredients:

- 1 Boston butt
- 1 pale ale
- 2/3 cup Dijon or spicy mustard
- 1 tbsp brown sugar
- 1 tsp red pepper flakes
- 1 cup rice vinegar (apple cider or white distilled vinegar works too)
- 1 tsp liquid smoke

Directions:

In pot combine beer, mustard, brown sugar, red pepper flakes, vinegar, liquid smoke; put pork in brine, throw in ice cubes and set in refrigerator 4 hours to overnight

Set grill to 225 and cook 6-9 hours or until an internal temp of 195 is reached

Florida Butt

Sub Adobo powder for the soy sauce! Makes 1 butt

Ingredients:

- 1 Boston butt
- 1 dark beer
- 1 tbsp low sodium soy sauce
- ½ tbsp rice wine vinegar or distilled vinegar
- 2/3 tbsp spicy mustard
- 1/3 tsp cloves
- ½ tsp black pepper
- 2/3 cup molasses (optional)

Directions:

In large pot combine beer, soy sauce, vinegar, mustard, cloves, pepper; drop in butt and marinade 4 hours to overnight

Set grill temp to 225 and place butt fat side up so fat drains down and seasons; cook 6-10 hours, if desired open another beer and coat with every hour

If using molasses-prior to cooking combine beer, soy sauce, vinegar, mustard, cloves, and pepper and use as brine. Using same ingredients add molasses and bring to a boil, lower temp, cover pot, let simmer 30 minutes. Then, let cool and use as sauce!

Smoked Pork Loin

Also works in crockpot. Just fill halfway up loin! Makes 1 pork loin.

Ingredients:

- 1 pork loin
- 1/3 tsp cloves
- ½ tsp cinnamon
- ½ tsp allspice
- ½ tsp mustard powder
- 1 tsp chili powder
- ½ tsp turmeric
- 1 tsp chicken granules

Directions:

On parchment paper sprinkle cloves, cinnamon, allspice, mustard powder, chili powder, turmeric, chicken granules; spread out evenly and roll pork loin across until coated

Set grill to 225-250 and cook with hickory chips 6-10 hours

Apple Spice Pork Loin

For festive falls sandwiches, try pumpkin spice! Makes 1 pork loin

Ingredients:

- 1 pork loin
- ½ tbsp apple pie spice
- 1 tbsp brown sugar
- ½ cup crushed pecans
- 1 tbsp Worcestershire sauce

Directions:

Layout parchment paper, spread-out apple-pie spice, brown sugar, crushed pecans evenly, then roll loin through until coated.

Pour Worcestershire evenly across loin and wrap with clear wrap; let sit in refrigerator 3-4 hours

Set grill to 200 and grill until an internal temp of 195 is reached

Pork Chipotle Sliders

Top with pepper jack or queso! Makes 4 servings.

Ingredients:

- ½ pound ground pork
- 1 pinch salt and pepper
- ½ tsp chili powder
- 1 tbsp chipotle chiles, diced
- 1/2 tsp diced jalapeno (optional)
- 1 tbsp red onion, diced
- 1 tbsp chopped cilantro
- 1/2 tsp minced garlic
- 4 slices white cheddar cheese

Directions:

First, mix together chicken, salt & pepper, chili powder, diced chipotle peppers, onion, cilantro, garlic.

Form 4, 1-inch thick and grill over medium-high heat 4-5 minutes per side.

Next, during last minute of cooking top with cheese and let melt.

Place the chicken burgers on bun and enjoy.

Pork Onion & Jalapeno Burger

Also, great as sliders! Makes 2 servings.

Ingredients:

- ½ lb. ground pork
- 1/2 packet golden onion seasoning (such as Lipton's)
- ½ tsp pepper
- 1/3 cup julienned onions
- 2 tbsp chopped jalapenos
- Butter, for toasting buns
- 2 hamburger buns
- Thick steak sauce (examples: Heinz 57 or A1)

Directions:

Mix together the ground pork, onion seasoning, pepper, onions, jalapenos.

Form into 4, 1-inch thick patties.

Smear butter on bread and toast over indirect heat.

Grill burgers 4- 5minutes per side.

Place on bun and top with steak sauce.

Oven/Stove

Easy Stovetop Chops

If chops stick to a pan when going to flip, it means they are not done and need more time. Be patient! Makes 2 chops.

Ingredients:

- 2 tbsp butter
- ½ tbsp extra-virgin olive oil
- 1/4 tsp Himalayan salt
- 1/3 tsp black pepper
- 2 center cut, boneless pork chops
- Herb de Provence seasoning

Directions:

In skillet over high heat melt butter into olive oil and swirl around.

.Sprinkle pan with salt and pepper.

Cook/sear 3-5 minutes per side.

Juicy Pan-Fried Chops

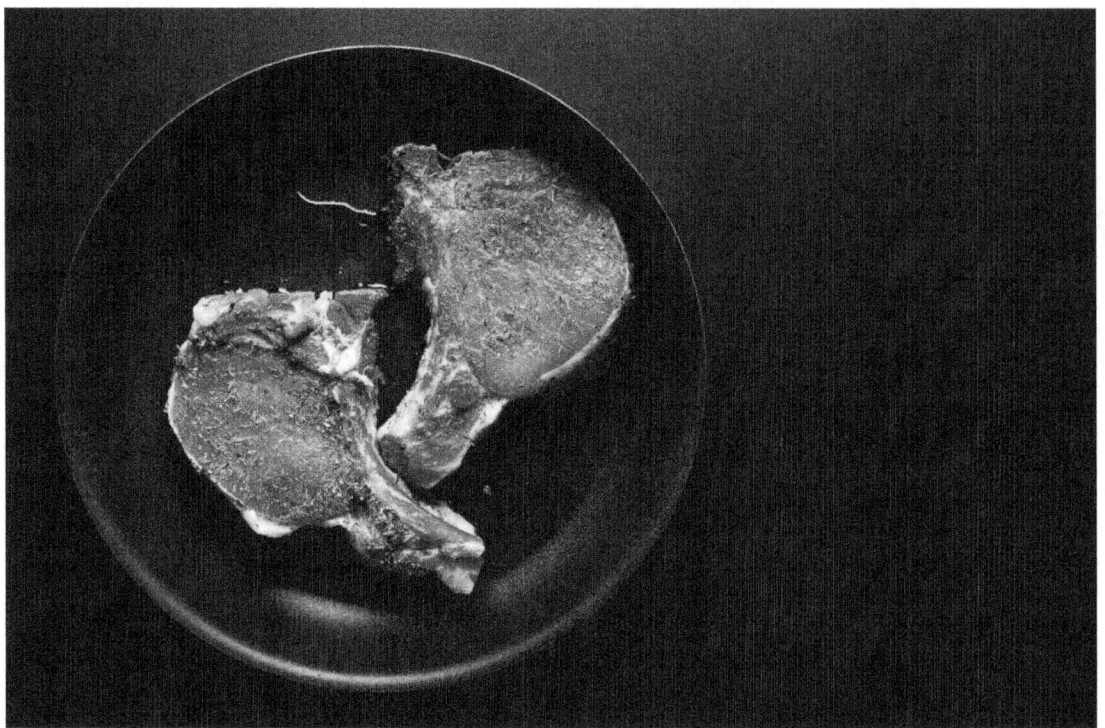

Easy & delicious! Makes 2 chops

Ingredients:

- 2 center cut, boneless pork chops
- ½ stick butter
- ½ tbsp olive oil
- 1 tbsp, minced or grated onion
- 1 tsp garlic, minced or grated
- 1 bouquet herbs
- 1/2 cup chicken broth or stock

Directions:

In skillet over medium-high heat melt butter into oil.

Add in onions, garlic and sauté 1 minute.

Stir in broth/stock and herbs. Slowly oscillate bouquet 30-40 seconds.

Add in chops, place face down and let cook 4-6 minutes per side.

Pork Tacos with an Avocado Salsa

For extra flavor, try adding chili pepper or paprika! Makes 4 servings.

Ingredients:

- 1 cup shredded pork
- 1/4 cup Mirepoix
- 2 avocados, diced
- 1 seedless cucumber, diced
- 1 tbsp cilantro
- 1 tbsp honey
- 1/4 tsp salt
- 1/4 cup chicken broth
- 1/3 cup water
- 2/3 tsp lemon juice
- 4 corn or flour 8-inch tortillas

Directions:

Mix together mirepoix, diced avocado, diced cucumber, diced cilantro, honey, salt, chicken broth, water, lemon juice.

Cover and chill.

In pot warm pork through.

Make pork tacos and top with salsa.

Pork Taquitos

Use leftover pork meat!!! Makes 4 taquitos

Ingredients:

- 4 10-inch flour tortillas
- 1 cup shredded pork
- 1/3 cup tomato sauce
- Italian seasoning
- ½ tbsp chili powder
- 1 package shredded cheddar cheese

Directions:

Preheat oven to 350. Prepare a 9x9 casserole dish

Mix together shredded pork, tomato sauce, Italian seasoning, chili powder, cheese.

Layout tortillas and spoon meat vertically down one side of the tortilla.

Bake 30 minutes.

Roasted Ranch Broccoli with Pork & Tofu Cubes

Works with cauliflower too! Makes 12 broccoli florets

Ingredients:

- 12 broccoli florets
- Olive oil spray
- 1 packet ranch seasoning
- 1 cup shredded cheddar cheese
- 1 onion julienned
- 1 tsp minced garlic
- 1 cup pork cubes, 1x1
- ½ package firm cubed tofu

Directions:

Pre-heat oven to 425 and line baking tray with aluminum foil on baking sheet. Fresh broccoli is best, but frozen will work if it is completely thawed it out.

Place florets on sheet.

Mix together seasoning, cheese, breadcrumbs.

Sprinkle over florets.

Cook 40-45minutes

In skillet sauté onion and garlic 1 minute.

Add in pork cubes and tofu cubes 1-2 minutes.

Pork & Beans Tater Tot Casserole

Great for kids and kids at heart! Makes 4 servings

Ingredients:

- 1 tbsp olive oil
- 1 onion, julienned or diced
- ½ cup tater tots
- 2 cans pork and beans
- ½ cup shredded pork
- 1 tbsp molasses
- 1 tbsp honey, organic
- ½ tbsp brown sugar
- 1/3 tsp cinnamon
- 1 tsp sweet paprika

- ½ tsp garlic powder and parsley
- 1 package shredded cheddar cheese

Directions:

Preheat oven to 350 and prepare 11x9 casserole dish.

Layout tater tots and onions in bottom of dish.

Mix together pork, beans, molasses, honey, brown sugar, cinnamon, sweet paprika, garlic powder with parsley.

Spread on top of tater tots and onions.

Top with cheese. Bake 30 minutes.

Faux Fried Pork Chops

Great flavor, half of the fat! Makes 2 servings.

Ingredients:

- Olive oil spray
- 2 chicken center cut pork chops
- 1 cup all-purpose flour
- ½ cup breadcrumbs

Directions:

Preheat oven to 425. Prepare a baking tray.

Thaw pork chops.

Next, coat both sides with flour and shake off excess.

Coat both sides with breadcrumbs. Then, shake off excess.

Bake 45 minutes to 1 hr. depending on the thickness.

Sweet and Spicy Hummus Pizza

Try different cheeses and spices! Makes 1 9" pizza.

Ingredients:

- 1 9" pizza shell
- 1 cup red pepper hummus
- 1 tbsp minced or grated onion
- ½ tbsp minced or grated garlic
- 1 cup petite diced tomatoes and juice
- 1/2 tsp smoked paprika
- 1/3 tsp cumin
- 1 tsp fennel
- ½ tsp cinnamon
- 1/2 cup shredded pork

- ¼ cup diced roasted red pepper
- 1/2 cup crumbled feta cheese

Directions:

Preheat oven as directed and prepare baking tray

Lay pizza shell on tray and spread on hummus.

Mix together onions, garlic, tomatoes, smoked paprika, cumin, fennel, cinnamon.

Spread evenly on hummus.

Top with shredded pork, roasted red pepper pieces, cheese.

Bake as directed.

Rosemary Pork & Sweet Potato

Try various fresh herbs! Makes 1 serving.

Ingredients:

- 1 cup rice, cooked
- 1 cup ground pork
- 1 cubed sweet potato
- ½ tbsp crushed walnuts
- 1/2 cup diced mushrooms
- ½ tbsp diced rosemary
- 1/3 tbsp diced parsley
- Shredded provolone for topping

Directions:

Fix rice into a bed on plate.

Sauté nuts, mushroom, rosemary, parsley 30-45 seconds.

Add in sweet potato and ground pork.

Warm through.

Spoon on top of rice.

Ginger Pork Stir-Fry

Also great with ground chicken or shrimp! Makes 2 servings.

Ingredients:

- 2 tbsp olive oil
- 1/2 tsp rice vinegar
- ½ tbsp diced onion
- ½ tsp minced garlic
- 1-2 drops chili oil (optional)
- ½ tsp chicken bouillon granules
- 1 piece ginger chopped
- 1 tbsp crushed walnuts
- ¼ cup diced or shredded chicken
- 1/2 cup cooked ramen (do not stir in seasoning packet)

Directions:

Preheat oven to 350 and prepare 8x8 pan.

Warm skillet over high heat and toast walnuts until fragrant.

In bowl whisk together oil, vinegar, onion, garlic, chili oil, bouillon granules and ginger.

Pour oil mixture in skillet.

Let chicken pieces sit 2 minutes before moving. They should be a nice golden brown, flip, repeat.

Pour in cooked ramen and toss.

Top with walnuts.

Breakfast Flatbread

Try it with agave or maple syrup! Makes 1 flatbread.

Ingredients:

- 1/3 cup shredded, diced, or 1/2 cup ground
- 2 eggs, beaten
- 2 cups spinach
- 1/3 cup onions, julienned
- ½ tbsp minced or grated garlic
- 1 large piece flatbread

Directions:

Preheat oven to 400 and prepare baking tray.

Warm skillet over medium high heat.

In a bowl whisk together pork, eggs, spinach, onions, garlic, turmeric.

Scramble then spoon onto flatbread.

Bake 12-15 minutes.

Italian Pork Chops and Roasted Potatoes

Pair with roasted veggies! Makes 2 servings.

Ingredients:

- 2 pork chops
- 2/3 cup breadcrumbs
- 1 tbsp Italian seasoning
- Olive oil for drizzling or spraying
- 10 small red potatoes

Directions:

Preheat oven to 400. Then, line baking tray with foil or parchment paper.

Coat chops with breadcrumbs and Italian seasoning.

Place in center of baking tray.

Cut potatoes in half and lay around the edges of tray.

Spray/drizzle chops and potatoes with olive oil and cook 40 minutes.

Check for doneness. If pork is pink or running unclear juices cook longer.

Spicy Sesame Pork Soup

Great pressure cooker meal! Makes 2 servings.

Ingredients:

- ½ tsp 5-spice powder
- 1 tsp sesame oil
- ½ tsp onion powder
- 1 cup ground pork
- 1 tsp garlic, minced
- 1/4 cup matchstick carrots
- ½ tbsp tomato paste
- 1 cup worth rice noodles
- ½ tsp diced thyme
- 1/3 cup vegetable or beef stock
- 1 tsp cornstarch

Directions:

In pot combine 5-spice powder, sesame oil, onion powder, pork, matchstick carrots, tomato paste, noodles, oregano, stock.

Stir in cornstarch.

Bring to a boil. Then, reduce heat and cover. Simmer for 15-20 minutes.

Easy Eggroll Wrappers and Pork Filling

Oh, so worth it! Makes 12-18 egg rolls

Ingredients:

- 1 1/3 cups cornstarch (coconut flour, potato starch, tapioca flour or anything similar works)
- 1 1/3 cups brown rice flour (can sub with g.f. white or oat flour)
- 1/3 tsp xanthan gum (if not already in the flour)
- 1/4 tsp salt
- 2 eggs
- 3/4 cup water
- 1 cup ground pork
- 1 tsp paprika
- ½ tsp pepper
- 2 tbsp Mire Poix

- ¼ cup shredded purple cabbage

Directions:

Combine starch, flour, gum, salt.

Whisk together eggs and water then pour into starch mix.

Stir until dough forms a ball.

Sprinkle counter/work surface with starch and roll 1/3 dough to preferred thickness (we opted for approx. ¼-inch thick.

Cut into 6x6 sections and place on prepared baking sheet.

Next, cover with damp towel and store in a cool, dark place.

In pot combine ground pork, paprika, pepper, and brown then drain.

Let pot cool and wipe out.

Place pork back into pot and stir in mire poix and cabbage.

Spoon mixture into egg rolls.

Lastly, fry 1-2 minutes per side or until golden brown.

Pork Thyme Eggrolls

Try as spring rolls! Makes 20 servings.

Ingredients:

- ¼ tsp rice vinegar
- 1/4 cup olive oil
- 1-2 drops chili oil or paste
- ½ tbsp thyme
- 1 tsp minced garlic
- 1 tsp minced or grated onion
- ½ tbsp shredded carrots
- 2 diced scallions

- 2/3 cup shredded purple cabbage
- 1 tsp red pepper flakes (optional)
- ½ lb. ground pork, browned
- 20 eggroll wrappers

Directions:

In skillet mix olive oil, wine vinegar, chili oil, thyme, garlic, onion.

Cover and chill in fridge at least 5 minutes (the longer the better).

Next, in bowl mix together carrots, scallions, cabbage, red pepper flakes, browned pork.

Spoon into wrappers.

Lastly, fry 1-2 minutes per side or until golden brown.

Pork Enchiladas

An easy lunch! Makes 4 servings

Ingredients:

- 2 cups shredded or ground pork
- 2-4 cups petite diced tomatoes
- 1/2 tbsp minced garlic
- 1 tbsp diced onions
- 1 tsp paprika
- 2/3 tsp chili powder
- ½ tsp cumin
- 1 package 8-inch corn tortillas
- Shredded Mexican cheese or Monterey jack

Directions:

Preheat oven to 350. Prepare a 9x9 dish

Mix together tomatoes, paprika, chill powder, cumin, onions, garlic.

Lay down tortillas in bottom of dish, top with browned pork, 1/3-1/2 cup sauce, handful of cheese; repeat until full.

Bake 30 minutes

Baked Pork Nuggets and Sweet Potato Spirals

Easily converted to the crockpot! Makes 2 servings.

Ingredients:

- 1 turkey breast or tenderloin sliced into "nuggets"
- 1-2 cups sweet potato spirals
- 2 tbsp e.v olive oil
- 1 tsp grated onion
- ½ tsp minced garlic
- ¼ tsp finely diced oregano
- ½ tsp diced thyme
- 1 tsp cracked peppercorns
- 1/3 tsp ginger

Directions:

Preheat oven to 350 and line baking tray with aluminum foil or parchment paper.

While waiting, combine in airtight container oil, onion, garlic, oregano, thyme, peppercorns, ginger.

Next, place in fridge and chill until ready to serve. (the longer the better)

Layout pork "nuggets" and bake 20-30 minutes.

Lastly, divide spirals and top with vinaigrette and pork nuggets.
Serve.

Zesty Pork & Lentil Stew

Try various cheeses! Makes 2-4 servings

Ingredients:

- 2 tbsp extra virgin olive oil
- ½ tbsp red wine vinegar
- 1/3 cup + 1 tbsp beef stock or broth
- 1 cup browned and drained ground or shredded pork
- 1 cup lentils
- 1 tsp chopped shallot
- 2 diced cloves garlic
- 2-3 bay leaf
- ½ tsp jalapeno powder
- 1 cup diced tomatoes with green chilies
- ¼ cup chopped parsley

Directions:

In Dutch Oven combine e.v.o.o., vinegar, broth or stock, pork, lentils, shallot, garlic, bay leaves, jalapeno powder, tomatoes.

Cook 15-20 minutes.

Chops with an Avocado Portobella Sauce

Try various mushrooms! Makes 2 servings.

Ingredients:

- 2 pork chops
- 1 cup panko
- Olive oil spray
- 1/4 cup avocado oil
- ½ tbsp onions
- ½ tsp minced garlic
- ½ tbsp chopped rosemary
- ¼ cup cubed portobello mushrooms
- ¼ cup baby spinach

- ½ cup diced tomatoes
- 1/2 tbsp tomato paste
- 1 tbsp honey

Directions:

Preheat oven to 400 and prepare baking tray.

Bread chops & lay on tray at least 1-inch apart. Bake 40-50 minutes.

In medium or large pot, add avocado oil, onions, and garlic and sauté 2-3 minutes.

Add in chopped rosemary, mushrooms cube, spinach, tomatoes, paste, and honey.

Warm through

Simple Mediterranean Pasta

Any forms of pasta are ok! Makes 2 servings!

Ingredients:

- 1 cup ground or shredded pork, browned and drained
- 4 oz bowtie pasta
- 1/3 cup extra virgin olive oil
- 2 cloves garlic, chopped
- 1/3 cup chopped oregano
- ½ cup halved cherry tomatoes
- 1/3 cup chopped scallions
- 1/3 cup baby corn
- 1/3 cup chopped water chestnuts
- 4 cups tomato & bell pepper broth

Directions:

In pot mix browned and drained pork, uncooked pasta, oil, garlic, oregano, tomatoes, scallion, baby corn, water chestnuts, broth.

Bring to boil. Then, reduce heat and cover. Simmer 20-25 minutes approximately.

Pork Chops with Artichoke Hearts

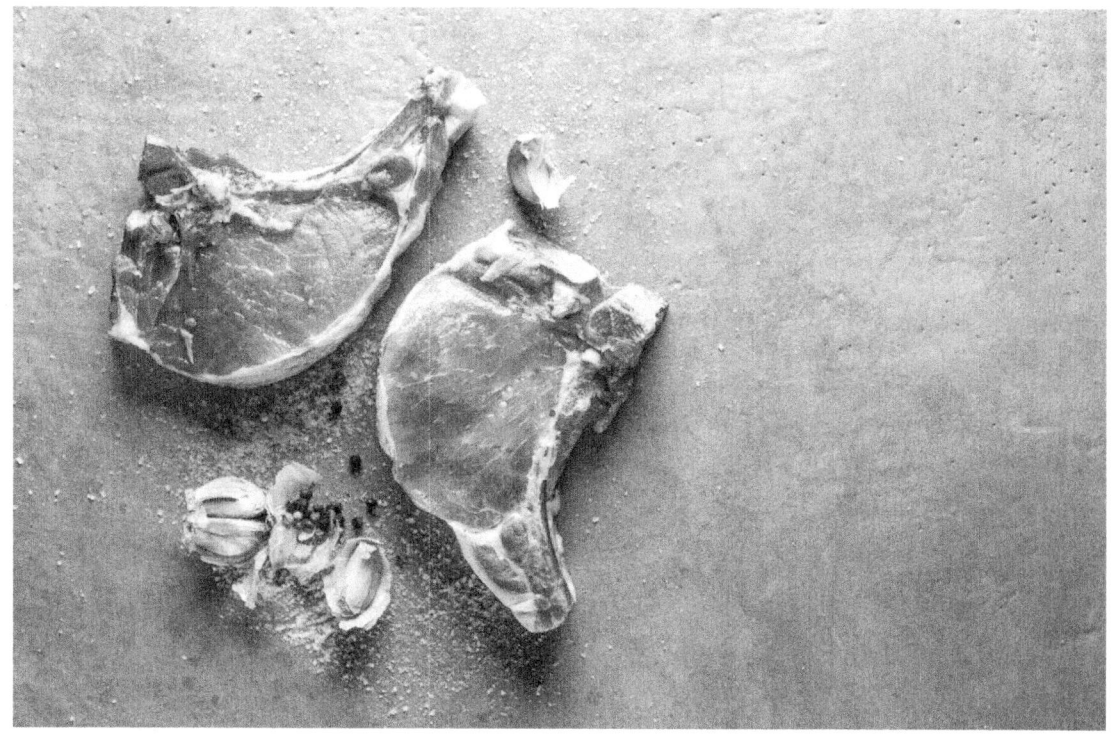

Sub brussels sprouts for the artichoke hearts! Makes 2 servings

Ingredients:

- 2 pork chops
- 3 oz artichoke hearts
- 1 tbsp olives, halved
- 6-8 chopped basil leaves
- 1/4 cup feta, crumbled
- 1 tsp red pepper flakes
- 1/3 tbsp balsamic vinegar
- ¼ cup water or chicken stock

Directions:

First, preheat oven to 400. Prepare baking sheet.

Place chops on baking tray and bake 35-45 minutes.

Next, in Dutch oven over medium high heat combine artichoke hearts, olives, basil leaves, feta, red pepper flakes, balsamic vinegar, and liquid.

Bring to boil, cover, reduce heat, simmer 20-30 minutes.

Kielbasa and Rice

Try it with apple-chicken sausage! Makes 2 servings

Ingredients:

- 1-2 cups sliced kielbasa
- ⅓ tbsp e.v. olive oil
- ½ tsp minced garlic
- 2 tbsp diced peppers and onions
- 1 tsp thyme
- 1/2 cup rice jasmine rice
- 1 cup water

Directions:

In skillet combine e.v. olive oil, kielbasa, onions and peppers, garlic, and thyme.

Stir around plate to disperse oils 30-45 seconds.

Add in sausage and sauté 30 seconds.

Add in rice and water.

Bring to a boil, cover, reduce temp, simmer 15-20 minutes.

Pork Pite

Pite means pie! Makes 2 servings.

Ingredients:

- 1 tsp e.v. olive oil
- 1/2 cup uncooked rice
- 1 cup ground pork, browned and drained
- 2 oz peas and carrots, washed and drained
- 2 tbsp diced red roasted peppers
- 1/2 tsp Italian seasoning
- ½ cup chicken stock
- 1 cup finely diced eggplant (sauté)
- 1 sheet phyllo dough
- 1 tub crumbled feta
- Honey for drizzling

Directions:

Preheat oven to 350 F. Line pan with parchment paper.

In pot combine olive oil, uncooked rice, ground turkey, peas and carrots, red roasted peppers, Italian seasoning, chicken stock.

Bring to boil, cover, reduce, simmer.

In another pot add olive oil and sauté eggplant for 3 minutes

Stack dough, brushing each layer with olive oil.

Cut a hole 6 inches in diameter and one sheet 7-inches in diameter.

Place the small stack on top of the largest sheet.

Sprinkle each with crumbled feta and top with eggplant.

Turn edge of bottom sheet up and press into small stack.

Bake for about 25-30 minutes approximately until phyllo is golden and base is stable.

Remove and let them cool.

Drizzle with honey before serving.

Pork Chops and Zucchini Fritters

Try corn or apple fritters! Makes 2 servings.

Ingredients:

- 10-12 pork medallions
- 1 tbsp olive oil
- 1/2 cup chickpeas
- 1 tsp chopped thyme
- 2 tbsp lemon juice
- 2-3 tbsp crumbled feta cheese
- 2 cups zucchini
- 2 eggs
- 1 onion finely diced
- 1 tbsp diced oregano
- 2 tbsp diced mint

- 1 tsp thyme
- 1/2 tsp pepper
- 1/3 cup breadcrumbs
- 1/3 tsp baking powder
- 1/2 cup flour
- Olive oil for frying

Directions:

In skillet cook medallions to internal temp of 145. Transfer to plate to drain.

In pot combine olive oil, chickpeas, thyme, lemon juice.

Divide between two bowls.

Top with feta cheese.

Combine onion, oregano, mint, thyme, pepper, baking powder, flour.

Beat in eggs one at a time.

Add in zucchini and toss well.

Spoon into 1-inch rounded spoonful's and fry 1-2 minutes per side or until golden brown.

Layout on paper towel and let drain.

Instant Pot/Crockpot

Instant Pot Spicy Pork Tacos

Also, great on flatbread! Makes 8 servings.

Ingredients:

- 1 cup ground pork
- 1/2 tsp fennel
- 1 tsp Sichuan pepper
- 1 cup petite diced tomatoes
- 1/4 cup diced onion
- 1/4 cup chopped parsley
- 1 tbsp diced oregano
- ¼ cup olive oil
- 1 tsp lemon peel
- 1/4 tsp pepper
- 3 cups torn Chinese lettuce

- 1/3 cup shredded provolone or white cheddar cheese
- 8 taco shells

Directions:

In pot mix together group pork, fennel, and pepper, brown approx. 2 minutes.

In separate bowl mix tomatoes, diced onions, chopped parsley, chopped oregano, olive oil, lemon peel, pepper, torn lettuce, cheese.

Cook on high 5 minutes.

QPR

Sesame Pork and Bok Choy

Wonderful! Makes 4 servings.

Ingredients:

- ½ tsp sesame oil
- 1 tbsp low sodium soy sauce
- ½ tsp garlic powder
- ½ lb. ground pork
- ½ pound asparagus, cut into 2-inch pieces
- 2-4 stalks bok choy sliced
- 2 Roma tomatoes sliced
- 1 tbsp e.v. olive oil
- 1/2 tbsp lemon juice

- 1/2 tsp grated lemon zest
- 1/3 tsp thyme
- ½ tsp diced basil
- 1 package cauliflower rice

Directions:

In pot brown pork and drain.

In pot combine sesame oil, soy sauce, garlic powder, asparagus, bok choy, tomatoes, olive oil, lemon juice, lemon zest, thyme,

Cook on high 5 minutes.

QPR

Pork and Black bean Pitas

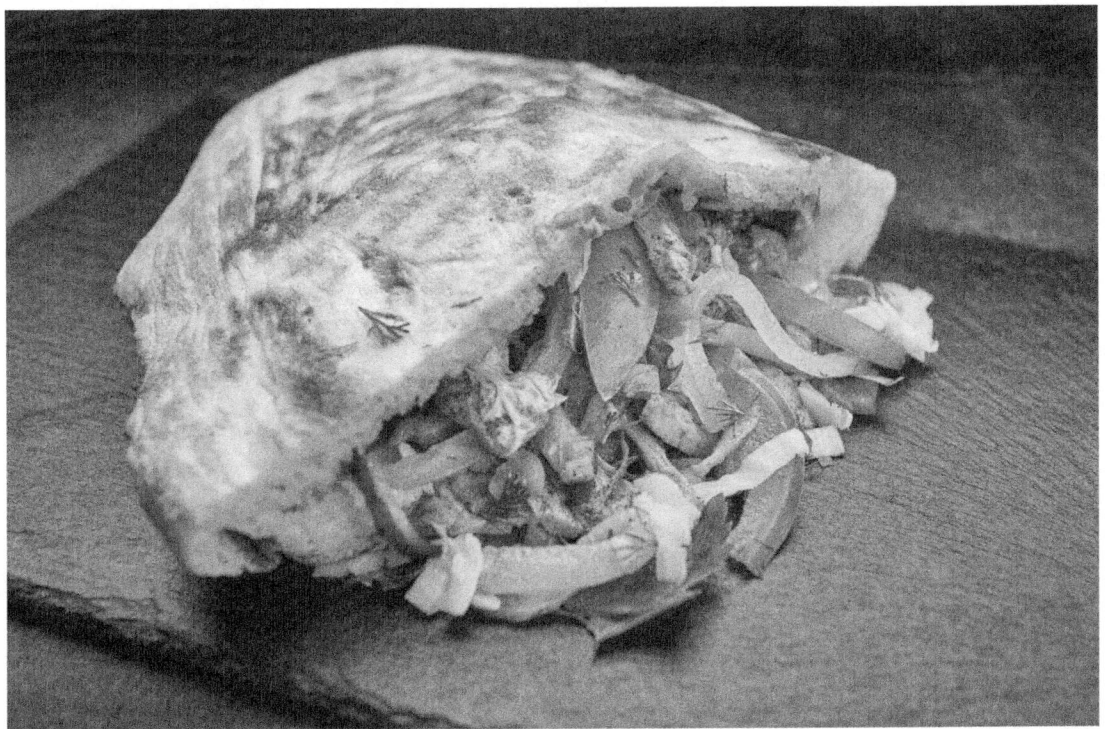

Or serve over rice! Makes 4 servings.

Ingredients:

- ½ lb. ground pork
- ½ block firm silken cubed tofu, pressed dry
- 1 can washed drained black beans
- 1 cup julienned sweet bell peppers
- 3/4 cup diced egg plant
- 4 quartered cherry tomatoes, halved
- 1/2 tbsp lemon juice
- 1/2 tsp grated lemon zest
- 1/4 cup grated Parmesan-Romano cheese

Directions:

In pot brown pork and drain

Combine tofu, black beans, bell peppers, eggplant, tomatoes, lemon juice, lemon peel, cheese.

Cook on high 5 minutes.

QPR

Instant Pot Pork Puttanesca

Also great with ground beef or ground turkey! Makes 2 servings.

Ingredients:

- 1 tbsp butter
- ½ onion diced
- ½-1 cup ground pork, browned and drained
- ½ tbsp garlic, minced
- ¼ cup grated carrots
- 1/3 cup tomato sauce
- 1 tbsp tomato paste
- 1 tbsp capers, drained
- 1 tsp red pepper flakes
- 1 cup cooked fettucine
- 1 tsp Italian seasoning

- Shredded provolone for topping

Directions:

In pot sauté olive oil, onions, browned and drained pork, garlic, carrots, tomato sauce, paste, capers, red pepper flakes, pasta, Italian seasoning.

QPR

Transfer to plates and top with cheese.

Chunked Pork Over Zucchini Spirals

Can sub with sweet potato spirals! Makes 1-2 servings.

Ingredients:

- 10 chunked pork
- ½ tsp sweet ginger
- ½ tsp turmeric
- 1-2 cups zucchini spirals, divided
- 2 tbsp e.v. olive oil
- 1/2 tbsp grated onion
- 1 tsp garlic, minced
- 1/2 cup tomato sauce
- 1/2 tsp tomato paste
- 1/4 tsp Italian seasoning
- 1/3 package firm, cubed tofu

Directions:

In pot mix pork chunks, sweet ginger, turmeric and sauté 2-3 minutes or until no longer pink.

Transfer to paper towel lined plate and drain.

In pot on sauté mode add olive oil and sauté onions, garlic, and tofu 1-2 minutes.

Stir in tomato sauce, paste, & Italian seasoning.

Toss in zucchini spirals.

Cook 4 minutes on high.

QPR

Printed in Dunstable, United Kingdom